W9-DAT-268

THE APPLE TREE

The Apple Tree

CHRISTMAS MUSIC FROM THE CAMBRIDGE HYMNAL

EDITED BY
DAVID HOLBROOK AND ELIZABETH POSTON

CAMBRIDGE UNIVERSITY PRESS

CAMBRIDGE

LONDON · NEW YORK · MELBOURNE

Published by the Syndics of the Cambridge University Press
The Pitt Building, Trumpington Street, Cambridge CB2 IRP
Bentley House, 200 Euston Road, London NWI 2DB
32 East 57th Street, New York, NY 10022, USA
296 Beaconsfield Parade, Middle Park, Melbourne 3206, Australia

This collection:
© Cambridge University Press 1976

First published 1976

Printed in Great Britain
at the
University Printing House, Cambridge
(Euan Phillips, University Printer)

Library of Congress Cataloguing in Publication Data
Main entry under title:
The Apple tree.
Includes index.
1. Christmas music. 2. Hymns, English.
I. Holbrook, David. II. Poston, Elizabeth,
1905–   . III. Title. IV. Title: The
Cambridge hymnal.
M2065.A7   783.9'52   76–12916
ISBN 0 521 29116 X paperback
ISBN 0 521 21479 3 hard covers

CONTENTS

M 2065
.A7
1976

SwTS

Preface vii
Acknowledgements ix

1 Jesus Christ the Apple Tree 2
2 Deo Gratias 4
3 A Virgin Most Pure 6
4 Chanticleer's Carol 8
5 Behold a Silly Tender Babe 10
6 The Boar's Head Carol 12
7 Corpus Christi Carol (Down in Yon Forest) 14
8 The First Nowell 18
9 Francis Kindlemarsh's Carol 20
10 God Rest You Merry 22
11 Hark, the Herald-Angels Sing 24
12 The Holly and the Ivy 26
13 Watts's Cradle Song 30
14 I Sing of a Maiden 32
15 In a Field As I Lay 34
16 In the Bleak Mid-Winter 36
17 Poor Little Jesus 38
18 Where Riches Is Everlastingly 42
19 I Sing the Birth 45
20 Jesus Born in Beth'ny 46
21 Christmas Day 52
22 Lullay, Lullay, Thou Lytil Child 53
23 Lullay My Liking 54

24 Nowell, Nowell, Nowell 56
25 Balulalow (O My Deir Heart) 61
26 Adeste Fideles 62
27 The Sussex Carol 64
28 Qui Creavit Coelum 66
29 Sing, All Men 68
30 Sweet Was the Song (Virgin's Lullaby) 72
31 That Lord That Lay in Asse Stall 76
32 Coverdale's Carol 78
33 The Virgin Mary Had a Baby Boy 82
34 There Is No Rose of Such Virtue 1 84
35 There Is No Rose of Such Virtue 2 85
36 This Endris Night 86
37 My Dancing Day 1 88
38 My Dancing Day 2 90
39 What Tidings Bring'st Us, Messenger? 96
40 While Shepherds Watched 99
41 Wondrous Love 100
42 That Virgin's Child 103
43 The Holy Son of God Most High 104
44 A New Year Carol 106
45 Twelfth Night Song 108
46 Lord, When the Wise Men Came 112

Index 115

PREFACE

This book contains the carols and hymns for the Christmas season from the Cambridge Hymnal. The full Hymnal came into being because of a challenge issued to the 'words' editor by a group of teachers studying the teaching of poetry and English in general on a course in Cambridge. The teachers were concerned not only that the collections currently used in school assemblies or churches contained so much that was ugly and poor, but also much that was without meaning. Could a hymn book be produced in which every set of verses and every tune and arrangement was of the highest standard, in which words and music complemented each other, and meaning was an overall, guiding concern?

The Cambridge Hymnal is the result of ten years' literary and musical research, pursued in the spirit of this challenge – to renew the tradition of the English devotional lyric. Old forms, old melodies, appear as themselves and in settings seen afresh through twentieth-century eyes. New tunes, specially commissioned, appear beside the best of the traditional and the familiar. The editors see in all of them a harmony of words and music, and the meaning, vitality and directness which they seek to revive.

It is a collection containing hymns for congregational and non-congregational singing, some familiar and for all, others needing to be studied and learned. It presupposes the intelligent participation of the user in a new appraisal. What is new here is a new affirmation of standards and their application. Since songs are for singing, all have the common factor, whatever their range or type, of practical accessibility in performance – the right of the performers to enjoy taking part together.

These principles, literary, musical and devotional, inform the Christmas section of the Hymnal. It has already contributed to the improvement of our Christmas ceremonies, and the decision was taken to publish it separately in this format to make it more widely accessible. We hope we have succeeded in representing the long, strong and continuing native tradition of 'plain music well done'. We hope it will be used with full enjoyment in the celebration of Christmas in homes, churches, chapels and schools.

COPYRIGHT AND ACKNOWLEDGEMENTS

The list below covers every edition of the Cambridge Hymnal and specifies every item (words or music) in which rights are controlled by a copyright holder. Sources and other acknowledgements are also indicated in many cases in the body of the book. Items not listed here may be assumed to be out of copyright.

Performing and recording rights are reserved as part of the copyright, and are administered by the Performing Rights Society, the Mechanical Copyright Protection Society and affiliated bodies throughout the world. Application should be made to these societies for licenses to perform, etc.

The publishers and editors are grateful to the proprietors listed below for permission to use copyright material.

1 Setting by Elizabeth Poston © Elizabeth Poston 1967, performing and mechanical reproduction rights controlled by Cambridge University Press; other rights controlled by composer

2 Setting by Norman Fulton © Norman Fulton 1967, all rights controlled by Cambridge University Press

3 Arrangement by Elizabeth Poston © Elizabeth Poston 1967; performing and mechanical reproduction rights controlled by Cambridge University Press, other rights controlled by composer

4 Setting by Norman Fulton, © Norman Fulton 1967, all rights controlled by Cambridge University Press

5 Arrangement by Elizabeth Poston © Elizabeth Poston 1967; performing and mechanical reproduction rights controlled by Cambridge University Press, other rights controlled by composer

6 Traditional words and melody arranged by Elizabeth Poston © Elizabeth Poston 1967; performing and mechanical reproduction rights controlled by Cambridge University Press, other rights controlled by composer

7 Traditional words and melody collected by Ralph Vaughan Williams, published in his arrangement in *Eight Traditional Carols*, and reproduced by permission of the publishers, Stainer and Bell Ltd. New arrangement by Nicholas Maw first published in this Hymnal © Nicholas Maw 1967, all rights controlled by Cambridge University Press

8 Descant by Elizabeth Poston © Elizabeth Poston 1967, all rights controlled by Cambridge University Press

9 Arrangement by Michael Paget © 1967, all rights controlled by Cambridge University Press

10 Arrangement by Elizabeth Poston © Elizabeth Poston 1967; performing and mechanical reproduction rights controlled by Cambridge University Press, other rights controlled by composer

12 Folk carol melody collected by Cecil Sharp, reproduced by permission of Novello and Co. Ltd.; setting by Benjamin Britten (S.A.T.B.) copyright 1957 by Boosey and Hawkes Music Publishers Ltd.

13 Setting by Stanley Taylor © Stanley Taylor 1967, all rights controlled by Cambridge University Press

14 Setting by Lennox Berkeley © Lennox Berkeley 1967, all rights controlled by Cambridge University Press

15 Setting by Christopher Morris © Christopher Morris 1967, all rights controlled by Cambridge University Press

16 Setting by Gustav Holst © Miss Imogen Holst and the Trustees of the late Gustav Holst, by kind permission of the Trustees

17 Arrangement by Elizabeth Poston © Elizabeth Poston 1967; performing and mechanical reproduction rights controlled by Cambridge University Press, all other rights controlled by composer

18 Setting by Peter Warlock, copyright in U.S.A. and all countries 1928 by the Oxford University Press, London, reproduced by permission of the publishers

19 Setting by William Mathias © William Mathias 1967, all rights controlled by Cambridge University Press

20 Traditional Virginian words and melody

© John Jacob Niles collected by John Jacob Niles, reproduced by permission of the publishers, G. Schirmer Inc. Arrangement by Elizabeth Poston © Elizabeth Poston 1967, all rights controlled by Cambridge University Press

21 Words from *Collected Poems* by Andrew Young, © Rupert Hart Davis 1960, by permission of the publisher. Setting by Elizabeth Poston © Elizabeth Poston 1967, all rights controlled by Cambridge University Press

22 Setting by Alan Ridout © Alan Ridout 1967 all rights controlled by Cambridge University Press

23 Setting by Gustav Holst, reproduced by permission of the publishers, J. Curwen & Sons Ltd.

24 Words from a MS. in the Library of Trinity College, Cambridge, by permission of the Master and Fellows. Setting by Elizabeth Maconchy © Elizabeth Maconchy 1967, all rights controlled by Cambridge University Press

25 Scottish traditional melody arranged by Elizabeth Poston © Elizabeth Poston 1967; performing and mechanical reproduction rights controlled by Cambridge University Press, all other rights controlled by composer

26 Descant by Elizabeth Poston © Elizabeth Poston 1967, all rights controlled by Cambridge University Press

27 Traditional Sussex carol collected and arranged by R. Vaughan Williams in *Eight Traditional Carols* by permission of the publishers, Stainer and Bell Ltd. Adaptation by E. Harold Geer reproduced by permission of Yale University Press from *Hymnal for Schools and Colleges*

28 Harmonized by Anthony Milner © Anthony Milner 1967, all rights controlled by Cambridge University Press

29 Kentucky folk carol collected by John Jacob Niles, reproduced by permission of the publishers, G. Schirmer Inc., New York (Chappell and Co. Ltd., London). Arrangement by Elizabeth Poston © Elizabeth Poston 1967, all rights controlled by Cambridge University Press

30 Setting by Stanley Taylor © 1967 J. Curwen and Sons Ltd., 29 Maiden Lane, London, W.C.2

31 Setting by Imogen Holst © Imogen Holst 1967, all rights controlled by Cambridge University Press

32 Setting by Ralph Vaughan Williams (from *Hodie*) © Oxford University Press, by permission of the publishers

33 Words and melody reprinted from the Edric Connor collection *West Indian Spirituals and Folk Tunes*, by permission of Boosey and Hawkes Music Publishers Ltd. Arrangement by Elizabeth Poston © Elizabeth Poston 1967

34, 35 Words reproduced by permission of the Master and Fellows of Trinity College, Cambridge. Music originally transcribed and edited by John Stevens in *Musica Britannica* Vol. IV © the Royal Musical Association (agents Stainer and Bell Ltd.). Simplified version (35) edited by John Stevens, also by permission of Stainer and Bell Ltd.

36 Arrangement by Elizabeth Poston © Elizabeth Poston 1967; performing and mechanical reproduction rights controlled by Cambridge University Press, all other rights controlled by the composer

37, 38 Arrangement by Elizabeth Poston © Elizabeth Poston 1967; performing and mechanical reproduction rights controlled by Cambridge University Press, all other rights controlled by composer

39 Arrangement by Elizabeth Poston © Elizabeth Poston 1967, all rights controlled by Cambridge University Press

40 Melody in the tenor harmonization by Elizabeth Poston © Elizabeth Poston 1967; performing and mechanical reproduction rights controlled by Cambridge University Press, all other rights controlled by composer

41 Arrangement by Elizabeth Poston © Elizabeth Poston 1967, all rights controlled by Cambridge University Press

42 Setting by Edmund Rubbra reproduced by permission of Alfred Lengnick & Co. Ltd.

43 Arrangement by Elizabeth Poston © Elizabeth Poston 1967, all rights controlled by Cambridge University Press

44 Setting by Benjamin Britten © 1963 Boosey and Co. Ltd.; reprinted by permission of Boosey and Hawkes Music Publishers Ltd.

45 Setting by Elizabeth Maconchy © Elizabeth Maconchy 1967, all rights controlled by Cambridge University Press

46 Words, cento Percy Dearmer, by permission of the copyright holders, Oxford University Press. Harmonization and descant by Elizabeth Poston © Elizabeth Poston 1967, all rights controlled by Cambridge University Press

THE APPLE TREE

1   JESUS CHRIST THE APPLE TREE

ELIZABETH POSTON, 1905–

4-PART or UNISON ACC.

3 For hap-pi-ness I long have sought, And plea-sure dear-ly I have bought: For
4 I'm wear-y with my for-mer toil, Here I will sit and rest a-while: I'm

hap-pi-ness I long have sought, And plea-sure dear-ly I have bought: I
wear-y with my for-mer toil, Here I will sit and rest a-while: Un-

opt. ending last time acc. only

missed of all; but now I see 'Tis found in Christ the ap-ple tree.
der the sha-dow I will be, Of Je-sus Christ the ap-ple tree.

© E.P.

JESUS CHRIST THE APPLE TREE

1 The tree of life my soul hath seen,
  Laden with fruit, and always green:
  The trees of nature fruitless be
  Compared with Christ the apple tree.

2 His beauty doth all things excel:
  By faith I know, but ne'er can tell
  The glory which I now can see
  In Jesus Christ the apple tree.

3 For happiness I long have sought,
  And pleasure dearly I have bought:
  I missed of all; but now I see
  'Tis found in Christ the apple tree.

4 I'm weary with my former toil,
  Here I will sit and rest awhile:
  Under the shadow I will be,
  Of Jesus Christ the apple tree.

5 This fruit doth make my soul to thrive,
  It keeps my dying faith alive;
  Which makes my soul in haste to be
  With Jesus Christ the apple tree.

Anon, collection of Joshua Smith, New Hampshire, 1784

DEO GRATIAS

NORMAN FULTON, 1909–
Commissioned for *The Cambridge Hymnal*

Con moto ♩ = c.76
UNISON

1 Ad - am lay y-bound-en, Bound-en in a bond; Four thou-sand win-ter

rall. *a tempo*

Thought he not too long. 2 And all was for an ap-ple, An

ap-ple that he took, As clerk - ès find-en Writ - ten in their

rall.

a tempo

book. 3 Ne had the ap-ple tak-en been, The ap-ple tak-en been,

1 Adam lay ybounden,
  Bounden in a bond;
  Four thousand winter
  Thought he not too long.

2 And all was for an apple,
  An apple that he took,
  As clerkès finden
  Written in their book.

3 Ne had the apple taken been,
  The apple taken been,
  Ne had never our lady
  A-been heavenè queen.

4 Blessèd be the time
  That apple taken was.
  Therefore we moun singen
  Deo gratias!

Sloane MS., c. 15th century.

3 A VIRGIN MOST PURE

English traditional
Melody from W. Sandys' *Christmas Carols Ancient and Modern*, 1833
Arranged, E. P.

Flowing (one-in-a-bar stress) ♩ = c.108

A vir-gin most pure, as the pro-phets do tell,— Hath brought forth a— ba-by, as it hath be-fell, To be— our Re-deem-er from death, hell and sin, Which A-dam's trans-gress-ion hath wrap-pèd us in. *Aye and*

CHORUS

there-fore be_ mer-ry, re - joice_ and be you mer-ry, Set sor-rows a -

side; Christ Je - sus our Sav - iour was born_ on this tide.

© Elizabeth Poston

1 A Virgin most pure, as the prophets do tell,
Hath brought forth a baby, as it hath befell,
To be our Redeemer from death, hell, and sin,
Which Adam's transgression hath wrappèd us in:
    Aye and therefore be merry, rejoice and be you merry,
    Set sorrows aside;
    Christ Jesus our Saviour was born on this tide.

2 At Bethlem in Jewry a city there was,
Where Joseph and Mary together did pass,
And there to be taxèd with many one mo',
For Caesar commanded the same should be so:

3 But when they had entered the city so fair,
A number of people so mighty was there,
That Joseph and Mary, whose substance was small,
Could find in the inn there no lodging at all:

4 Then they were constrained in a stable to lie,
Where horses and asses they used for to tie;
Their lodging so simple they took it no scorn,
But against the next morning our Saviour was born.

5 The King of all kings to this world being brought,
Small store of fine linen to wrap him was sought;
And when she had swaddled her young son so sweet,
Within an ox-manger she laid him to sleep:

6 Then God sent an angel from heaven so high,
To certain poor shepherds in fields where they lie,
And bade them no longer in sorrow to stay,
Because that our Saviour was born on this day:

7 Then presently after the shepherds did spy
A number of angels that stood in the sky,
They joyfully talked, and sweetly did sing,
To God be all glory, our heavenly King:

Traditional; this version taken from Davies Gilbert,
'Some Ancient Christmas Carols,' 1822

7

4   CHANTICLEER'S CAROL

NORMAN FULTON, 1909–
Commissioned for *The Cambridge Hymnal*

Vigoroso quasi carillon (not slower than ♩ = 104)

1 All this night   shrill chan - ti - cleer   Day's pro-
2 Wake, O earth,   wake ev - e - ry - thing!   Wake and
3 Hail, O Son,   O bless - èd Light,   Sent in-

claim - ing trum - pet - er,   Claps his wings   and loud - ly
hear the joy I bring;   Wake and joy;   for all this
to the world by night!   Let thy rays   and hea - ven-ly

cries: Mor - tals, mor - tals, wake and rise!   See a won - der Heav'n is
night Hea - ven and ev - 'ry twink-ling light,   All a - maz - ing, Still stand
pow'rs Shine in these dark souls of ours;   For most du - ly Thou art

un - der; From the earth is ris'n a Sun Shines all night, though
gaz - ing. An-gels, Pow'rs and all that be, Wake, and joy this
tru - ly God and man, we do con-fess: Hail, O Sun of

repeats | *last time*
(molto rall. last time only)

day be done._____ (_____)
Sun to see._____ (_____)
Right - eous - ness._____ (_____)

(molto rall. last time only)

ff

1 All this night shrill chanticleer,
Day's proclaiming trumpeter,
  Claps his wings and loudly cries:
  Mortals, mortals, wake and rise!
    See a wonder
    Heaven is under;
From the earth is risen a Sun
Shines all night, though day be done.

2 Wake, O earth, wake everything!
Wake and hear the joy I bring;
  Wake and joy; for all this night
  Heaven and every twinkling light,
    All amazing,
    Still stand gazing.
Angels, Powers, and all that be,
Wake, and joy this Sun to see.

3 Hail, O Sun, O blessèd Light,
Sent into the world by night!
  Let thy rays and heavenly powers
  Shine in these dark souls of ours;
    For most duly
    Thou art truly
God and man, we do confess:
Hail, O Sun of Righteousness!

William Austin of Lincoln's Inn (d. 1633)
From 'A Handfull of Celestial Flowers,' manuscribed by Ralph Crane,
in 'Ancient English Christmas Carols,' Edith Rickert, 1910

5 BEHOLD A SILLY TENDER BABE

Tune from Corner's *Geistliche Gesangbuch*, 1625
Arranged, E. P.

With an easy, gentle swing

1 Be - hold a sil - ly ten - der babe In freez - ing win - ter
2 The inns are full, no man will yield This lit - tle pil - grim

night_____ In home - ly man - ger trem - bling lies; A -
bed;_____ But forced he is with sil - ly beasts In

las a pi - teous sight,_____ A - las a pi - teous sight._____
crib to shroud his head,_____ In crib to shroud his head._____

6 The per-sons in that poor at-tire His roy-al li-v'ries

MELODY UNIS.

wear,___ The prince him-self___ is come from heav'n, This

pomp is priz-èd there,___ This pomp is priz-èd there.___

© Elizabeth Poston

1 Behold a silly[1] tender babe
   In freezing winter night
 In homely manger trembling lies;
   Alas a piteous sight.

2 The inns are full, no man will yield
   This little pilgrim bed;
 But forced is he with silly beasts
   In crib to shroud his head.

3 Despise him not for lying there:
   First what he is enquire:
 An orient pearl is often found
   In depth of dirty mire.

4 Weigh not his crib, his wooden dish,
   Nor beasts that by him feed;
 Weigh not his mother's poor attire
   Nor Joseph's simple weed.

5 This stable is a Prince's court,
   The crib his chair of state:
 The beasts are parcel of his pomp,
   The wooden dish his plate.

6 The persons in that poor attire
   His royal liv'ries wear,
 The prince himself is come from heaven,
   This pomp is prizèd there.

7 With joy approach, O Christian wight,
   Do homage to the King;
 And highly praise his humble pomp
   Which he from heaven doth bring.

Robert Southwell, c. 1561–1595. From 'New Prince, New Pompe'

[1] *silly* = simple, naïve, innocent.

11

6   THE BOAR'S HEAD CAROL

Traditional, Queen's College, Oxford (Brit. Mus. MS. Add. 5665)
Arranged, E. P.

At a moderate pace, broad and steady

Descant for 1 or 2* instruments and/or voices

1 The boar's head in hand bear I, Be-
2 The boar's head, as I un - der - stand, Is the

decked with bays and rose - ma - ry; And I
rar - est dish in all the land When

pray you my mas - ters, be mer - ry, *Quot*
thus be - decked with a gay gar - land, Let

es - tis in con - vi - vi - o:
us ser - vi - re can - ti - co:

* Suitable for trumpet.

CHORUS   (*Inst.*)

Ca - put a - pri de - fe - ro,   Red - dens lau - des Do - mi - no.

ALTERNATIVE CHORUS

Ca - put a - pri de - fe - ro,   Red - dens lau - des Do - mi - no.

MELODY

(The tenor part may be omitted if desired)

© Elizabeth Poston

1 The boar's head in hand bear I,
  Bedecked with bays and rosemary;
  And I pray you, my masters, be merry,
     Quot estis in convivio:[1]

   Caput apri defero,
   Reddens laudes Domino.[2]

2 The boar's head, as I understand,
  Is the rarest dish in all the land
  When thus bedecked with a gay garland,
     Let us *servire cantico:*[3]

3 Our steward hath provided this
  In honour of the King of bliss,
  Which on this day to be servèd is,
     In Reginensi atrio:[4]

Queen's College, Oxford, version;
first printed in Wynkyn de Worde's 'Christmasse Caroles', 1521

[1] *Quot*, etc.   So many as are in the feast.
[2] *Caput*, etc.   The boar's head I bring, giving praises to God.
[3] *Servire*, etc.   Serve with a song.
[4] *In*, etc.   In the Queen's hall.

7 CORPUS CHRISTI CAROL
(Down in Yon Forest)

Collected in Derbyshire by R. Vaughan Williams
Arranged by NICHOLAS MAW, 1935–
Commissioned for *The Cambridge Hymnal*

© WITH DESCANT *(verses 3 & 6)*

p dolce

3 At the bed - side___ there lies___ a stone: } *The*
6 O - ver that bed___ the moon___ shines bright: }

bells___ of Pa - ra - dise I heard them ring: } *Which the*
not - ing our Sav - iour was born___ this night. } *De -*

sweet Vir - gin Ma - ry knelt___ up - on: } *And I*

love my Lord Je - sus a - bove an - y - thing.

bove an - y - thing.

Meno mosso

Words and melody by permission of Stainer & Bell Ltd.

1 Down in yon forest there stands a hall:
  The bells of Paradise I heard them ring:
  It's covered all over with purple and pall:
  And I love my Lord Jesus above anything.

2 In that hall there stands a bed:
  It's covered all over with scarlet so red:

3 At the bed-side there lies a stone:
  Which the sweet Virgin Mary knelt upon:

4 Under that bed there runs a flood:
  The one half runs water, the other runs blood:

5 At the bed's foot there grows a thorn:
  Which ever blows blossom since he was born:

6 Over that bed the moon shines bright:
  Denoting our Saviour was born this night:

Derbyshire Traditional, collected with the music

8

THE FIRST NOWELL

English traditional melody
Harmony adapted from JOHN STAINER, 1840–1901
Descant, E. P.

Brisk and cheerful

The first Now-ell the an-gel did say Was to cer-tain poor shep-herds in fields as they lay; In fields where they lay, keep-ing their sheep, In a cold win-ter's night that was so deep: Now-ell, Now-ell, Now-ell, Now-ell, Born is the King of Is-ra-el.

DESCANT REFRAIN

Fine

MELODY

repeat REFRAIN

1 The first Nowell the angel did say
  Was to certain poor shepherds in fields as they
                                                lay;
  In fields where they lay, keeping their sheep,
  In a cold winter's night that was so deep:

  Nowell, Nowell, Nowell, Nowell,
  Born is the King of Israel!

2 They lookèd up and saw a star,
  Shining in the east, beyond them far;
  And to the earth it gave great light,
  And it continued both day and night:

3 And by the light of that same star,
  Three Wise Men came from country far;
  To seek for a king was their intent,
  And to follow the star wheresoever it went:

4 This star drew nigh to the north west;
  O'er Bethlehem it took its rest,
  And there it did both stop and stay
  Right over the place where Jesus lay:

5 Then did they know assuredly
  Within that house the King did lie:
  One entered in then for to see,
  And found the babe in poverty:

6 Then entered in those Wise Men three,
  Fell reverently upon their knee,
  And offered there in his presènce
  Both gold and myrrh and frankincense:

7 Between an ox-stall and an ass
  This child truly there born he was;
  For want of clothing they did him lay
  All in a manger, among the hay:

8 Then let us all with one accord
  Sing praises to our heavenly Lord,
  That hath made heaven and earth of nought,
  And with his blood mankind hath bought:

9 If we in our time shall do well,
  We shall be free from death and hell;
  For God hath preparèd for us all
  A resting place in general:

Traditional, from W. Sandys, 'Christmas Carols Ancient and Modern', 1833

FRANCIS KINDLEMARSH'S CAROL

Melody and bass by Orlando Gibbons, 1583–1625
Additional parts and descant by Michael Paget, 1936–
Commissioned for *The Cambridge Hymnal*

SONG 24

Moderately slow

From vir - gin's womb this Christ-mas day did spring____

____ The pre - cious seed that on - ly sav - èd man:

(v.2)

This day let____ man re - joice and sweet - ly sing____

____ Since on this day____ sal - va - tion first be - gan.

This day did____ Christ man's soul from death re - move,____

With glo-rious saints to dwell in heav'n a-bove.

last line, verse 4 only
DESCANT

The joy of Christ's birth on this day re-cite.

1 From virgin's womb this Christmas day did spring
   The precious seed that only savèd man:
This day let man rejoice and sweetly sing
   Since on this day salvation first began.
      This day did Christ man's soul from death remove,
      With glorious saints to dwell in heav'n above.

2 This day to man came pledge of perfect peace:
   This day to man came love and unity:
This day man's grief began for to cease,
   This day did man receive a remedy
      For each offence and ev'ry deadly sin
      That he, with guilty heart, has wandered in.

3 Now in Christ's flock let love be surely placed:
   Now from Christ's flock let concord hate expel:
Now of Christ's flock let love be so embraced,
   As we in Christ, and Christ in us may dwell.
      Christ is the author of all unity,
      From whence proceedeth all felicity.

4 O sing unto this glittering glorious King:
   O praise his name let every living thing:
Let heart and voice like bells of silver ring
   The comfort that this Christmas day did bring.
      Let lute and harp, with sound of sweet delight
      The joy of Christ's birth on this day recite.

'A Carowle for Christmas Day,' by Francis Kindlemarsh (fl. c. 1570),
from 'Songs of Sundry Natures,' by William Byrd (1589)

GOD REST YOU MERRY

Traditional English melody, from W. Sandys,
Christmas Carols Ancient and Modern, 1833
Arranged, E. P.

God rest you mer - ry, Gen - tle - men, Let no - thing you dis -
may, For Je - sus Christ our Sav - iour Was
born up - on this day, To save us all from
Sa - tan's pow'r When we were gone a - stray:

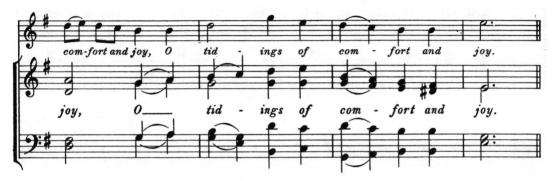

© Elizabeth Poston

1 God rest you merry, Gentlemen,
   Let nothing you dismay,
For Jesus Christ our Saviour
   Was born upon this day,
To save us all from Satan's power
   When we were gone astray:

   O tidings of comfort and joy.

2 In Bethlehem in Jewry
   This blessèd babe was born,
And laid within a manger,
   Upon this blessèd morn;
The which his mother Mary
   Nothing did take in scorn:

3 From God our heavenly Father
   A blessèd angel came,
And unto certain shepherds
   Brought tidings of the same,
How that in Bethlehem was born
   The Son of God by name:

4 'Fear not,' then said the angel,
   'Let nothing you affright,
This day is born a Saviour,
   Of virtue, power, and might;
So frequently to vanquish all
   The friends of Satan quite:'

5 The shepherds at those tidings
   Rejoicèd much in mind,
And left their flocks a-feeding,
   In tempest, storm and wind,
And went to Bethlehem straightway
   This blessèd babe to find:

6 But when to Bethlehem they came,
   Whereat this infant lay,
They found him in a manger,
   Where oxen feed on hay;
His mother Mary kneeling,
   Unto the Lord did pray:

7 Now to the Lord sing praises,
   All you within this place,
And with true love and brotherhood
   Each other now embrace;
This holy tide of Christmas
   All others doth deface:

Traditional, from Sandys, 1833

23

11 HARK, THE HERALD-ANGELS SING

Adapted from a Chorus of FELIX MENDELSSOHN-BARTHOLDY, 1809–47
by W. H. CUMMINGS, 1831–1915
Descant, E. P.

MENDELSSOHN

1 Hark, the he-rald-an-gels sing 'Glo-ry to the new-born
2 Christ, by high-est heav'n a - dored, Christ, the e - ver-last-ing

King; Peace on earth, and mer-cy mild, God and sin-ners re-con-
Lord, Late in time be-hold him come, Off-spring of the Vir-gin's

ciled!' Joy - ful, all ye na-tions, rise, Join the tri-umph of the
womb; Veiled in flesh the God-head see, Hail, the in-car-nate De-i-

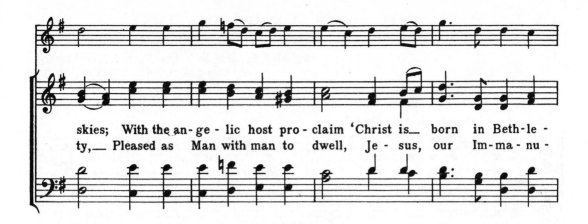

skies; With the an - ge - lic host pro - claim 'Christ is_ born in Beth - le -
ty,_ Pleased as Man with man to dwell, Je - sus, our Im - ma - nu -

hem.' } Hark! the he - rald - an - gels sing, 'Glo - ry to the new-born King.'
ell }

1 Hark, the herald-angels sing
   'Glory to the new-born King;
   Peace on earth, and mercy mild,
   God and sinners reconciled!'
   Joyful, all ye nations, rise,
   Join the triumph of the skies;
   With the angelic host proclaim
   'Christ is born in Bethlehem.'

2 Christ, by highest heaven adored,
   Christ, the everlasting Lord,
   Late in time behold him come,
   Offspring of the Virgin's womb.
   Veiled in flesh the Godhead see,
   Hail, the incarnate Deity,
   Pleased as Man with man to dwell,
   Jesus, our Immanuel!

Hark the herald-angels sing,
'Glory to the new-born King.'

3 Hail the heaven-born Prince of Peace!
   Hail, the Sun of Righteousness!
   Light and life to all he brings,
   Risen with healing in his wings;
   Mild he lays his glory by,
   Born that man no more may die,
   Born to raise the sons of earth,
   Born to give them second birth:

Charles Wesley, 1707–88,
altered by George Whitefield, 1714–70, Martin Madan, 1726–90, and others

12 THE HOLLY AND THE IVY

S.A.T.B.

English folk carol melody collected, Cecil Sharp
Arranged, BENJAMIN BRITTEN, 1913–

The verses should be sung at a more relaxed tempo than the
refrain. The solos can also be sung by chorus or semi-chorus

12 (continued)

all the trees that grows in woods The hol-ly bears the crown.

— the— hol - ly— bears crown.

REFRAIN
SOPRANO
ALTO
The ri-sing of the sun,— The run-ning of the— deer, The—
TENOR

BASS

play-ing of the— mer-ry harp, Sweet sing-ing in the choir.

By permission of Boosey & Hawkes. ©

1 The holly and the ivy
    Are trees that's both well known;
Of all the trees that grows in woods,
    The holly bears the crown.

    The rising of the sun,
    The running of the deer,
    The playing of the merry harp,
    Sweet singing in the choir.

2 The holly bears a blossom
    As white as any flower;
And Mary bore sweet Jesus Christ
    To be our sweet Saviour.

3 The holly bears a colour
    As green as any tree;
And Mary bore sweet Jesus Christ
    To set poor sinners free.

4 The holly bears a berry
    As red as any blood,
And Mary bore sweet Jesus Christ
    To do poor sinners good.

5 The holly bears a prickle
    As sharp as any thorn;
And Mary bore sweet Jesus Christ
    At Christmas day in the morn.

6 The holly bears a bark
    As bitter as any gall;
And Mary bore sweet Jesus Christ
    For to redeem us all.

7 The holly and the ivy
    Are trees that's both well known;
Of all the trees that grows in woods
    The holly bears the crown.

Traditional (adapted)

29

13 WATTS'S CRADLE SONG

STANLEY TAYLOR, 1902–72
Commissioned for *The Cambridge Hymnal*

Rather slow. Soft ♩ = 69
Instrumental (optional 8va)

Vocal

1 Hush! my dear, lie still and slum-ber; Ho-ly An-gels

guard thy bed! Heav'n-ly bless-ings _____ with-out num-ber

repeats   *last verse*

Gen-tly fall-ing on thy head. sing his praise.

humming and/or instrumental

UNISON

4 Soft and eas-y is thy cra-dle; Coarse and hard thy Sa-viour lay,
5 Lo, he slum-bers in his man-ger, Where the horn-èd ox-en fed;

When his birth-place was a sta-ble And his soft-est bed was hay.
Peace, my dar-ling! here's no dan-ger; Here's no ox a-near thy bed.

1 Hush! my dear, lie still and slumber;
 Holy Angels guard thy bed!
Heavenly blessings without number
 Gently falling on thy head.

2 Sleep, my babe; thy food and raiment,
 House and home, thy friends provide;
All without thy care and payment,
 All thy wants are well supplied.

3 How much better thou'rt attended
 Than the Son of God could be
When from Heaven he descended
 And became a child like thee.

4 Soft and easy is thy cradle;
 Coarse and hard thy Saviour lay,
When his birthplace was a stable
 And his softest bed was hay.

5 Lo, he slumbers in his manger,
 Where the hornèd oxen fed;
Peace, my darling! here's no danger;
 Here's no ox a-near thy bed.

6 Mayst thou live to know and fear him,
 Trust and love him all thy days:
Then go dwell for ever near him,
 See his face and sing his praise.

Isaac Watts, 1674–1748

31

I SING OF A MAIDEN

Lennox Berkeley, 1903–
Commissioned for *The Cambridge Hymnal*

Slow

1 I sing of a maiden That is mak-e-less,
2 He came all so still-e There his moth-er was,

3 He came all so still-e To his moth-er's bowr,
4 He came all so still-e There his moth-er lay,
5 Moth-er and maid-en Was ne-ver none but she;

King of all king-es To her son she ches.
As dew in A-pril-le That fall-eth on the grass.

As dew in A-pril-le That fall-eth on the flowr.
As dew in A-pril-le That fall-eth on the spray.
Well may such a la-dy God-es moth-er be.

Alternative (UNISON)

(Org. Ped.)

alternative ending last verse

1 I sing of a maiden
   That is makèless,[1]
King of all kingès
   To her son she ches.[2]

2 He came all so stillè
   There his mother was,
As dew in Aprillè
   That falleth on the grass.

3 He came all so stillè
   To his mother's bowr,
As dew in Aprillè
   That falleth on the flowr.

4 He came all so stillè
   There his mother lay,
As dew in Aprillè
   That falleth on the spray.

5 Mother and maiden
   Was never none but she;
Well may such a lady
   Godès mother be.

15th century, from Sloane MS., 2593, as in 'Early English Lyrics,'
E. K. Chambers and F. Sidgwick, 1947.

[1] *makeless* = matchless.
[2] *ches* = chose.

15 IN A FIELD AS I LAY

SOLO SA/UNISON ACCOMPANIED OR
SOLI AND 4-PART CHORUS

CHRISTOPHER MORRIS, 1922–
Commissioned for *The Cambridge Hymnal*

thee I play and sing;———
yet my King of bliss;———

Thus rocked she her child:

lul - la - by.

(TENORS)
2nd Basses
——mm——————
à 2
lul - la - by.

After verse 2

SOPRANO SOLO

Rocked I my child.

By by, lul-la-by, By by, lul-la-by.—— *mm (hum)——*

By by, lullaby,
Rocked I my child.

1 In a field as I lay, methought I heard
  A maiden say and speak these wordés wild:
  My little son, with thee I play and sing;
  Thus rocked she her child:

2 Then marvelled I right sore of this,
  A maid to have a child, ewis;
  My sweetest son, and yet my King of bliss;
  Thus rocked she her child:

14th century (altered)

16

CRANHAM

GUSTAV HOLST, 1874–1934

In moderate time

Verses 2 and 3 run:

2 Our God, heav'n can - not hold him   Nor___ earth sus -
3 E - nough for him, whom che - ru - bim   Wor - ship night and

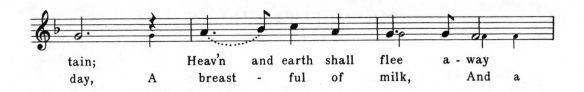

tain; Heav'n and earth shall flee a - way
day, A breast - ful of milk, And a

When he comes to reign: In the bleak mid -
man - ger full of hay; E - nough for him, whom

etc.

By kind permission of Miss Imogen Holst and the Trustees of the late Gustav Holst.

1 In the bleak mid-winter
   Frosty wind made moan,
Earth stood hard as iron,
   Water like a stone;
Snow had fallen, snow on snow,
   Snow on snow,
In the bleak mid-winter,
   Long ago.

2 Our God, heaven cannot hold him
   Nor earth sustain;
Heaven and earth shall flee away
   When he comes to reign:
In the bleak mid-winter
   A stable-place sufficed
The Lord God almighty,
   Jesus Christ.

3 Enough for him, whom cherubim
   Worship night and day,
A breastful of milk
   And a mangerful of hay;
Enough for him, whom angels
   Fall down before,
The ox and ass and camel
   Which adore.

4 What can I give him,
   Poor as I am?
If I were a shepherd
   I would bring a lamb;
If I were a wise man
   I would do my part;
Yet what I can I give him –
   Give my heart.

Christina Rossetti, 1830–94

17 POOR LITTLE JESUS

American traditional
Arranged, E. P.

2nd time D.S (v.4)

pi - ty and a shame, Lord, Lord,

Was-n't that a pi - ty and a shame?

1 It was poor little Jesus,
   Yes, yes;
   He was born on Christmas,
   Yes, yes;
   And laid in a manger,
   Yes, yes;
   Wasn't that a pity and a shame,
   Lord, Lord,
   Wasn't that a pity and a shame?

2 It was poor little Jesus,
   Child of Mary,
   Didn't have no cradle,

3 It was poor little Jesus,
   They nailed him to the cross, Lord,
   They hung him with a robber,

4 It was poor little Jesus,
   He's risen from darkness,
   He's 'scended into glory,
   No more a pity and a shame.

American traditional (slightly adapted).
Collected from coloured children in New York State and
printed in W. W. Newell, 'Songs and Games of American Children,' 1884–1911

18 WHERE RICHES IS EVERLASTINGLY
(Into this world this day did come)

PETER WARLOCK, 1894–1930

Fast, with a good swing

1 In - to this world this day did come
2 He that was rich with-out an - y need Ap-
*3 A sta - ble was his cham-ber, a cratch was his bed, He
4 A no - ble les - son here is us taught, To

Je - sus Christ, both God and man,
pear'd in this world in right poor weed To
had not a pil-low to lay un - der his head; With
set all world - ly rich - es at naught, But

Lord and Ser - vant in one per - son,
make us, that were poor in - deed,
maid - en's milk that Babe was fed, In
pray we that we may be thith - er brought Where

* Verse 3 may be sung as a solo, with harmonized chorus ad lib.
Copyright in U.S.A. and all countries, 1928, by the Oxford University Press, London

Born of the bless - ed Vir - gin Ma - ry.
Rich with - out an - y need tru - ly.
poor clothes was lap - ped the Lord Al - migh - ty.
rich - es is ev - er - last - ing - ly.

I pray you be mer - ry and sing with me In

wor - ship of Christ's na - ti - vi - ty. I pray you be mer - ry and

sing with me In wor - ship of Christ's na - ti - vi - ty.

HARMONIZED REFRAIN ad lib. Verse 3

I pray you be mer-ry ·and sing with_ me In_ wor-ship of Christ's na - ti - vi - ty.

Verse 3

last verse

- ti - vi - ty.

1 Into this world this day did come
Jesus Christ, both God and man,
Lord and Servant in one person,
Born of the blessed Virgin Mary.
I pray you be merry and sing with me
In worship of Christ's nativity.

2 He that was rich without any need
Appear'd in this world in right poor weed,
To make us, that were poor indeed,
Rich without any need truly.

3 A stable was his chamber, a cratch[1] was his bed,
He had not a pillow to lay under his head;
With maiden's milk that Babe was fed,
In poor clothes was lapped the Lord Almighty.

4 A noble lesson here is us taught,
To set all worldly riches at naught,
But pray we that we may be thither brought
Where riches is everlastingly.

16th century. Balliol College, Oxford, MS. 354

[1] *cratch* = crèche, crib or manger.

WILLIAM MATHIAS, 1924–
Commissioned for *The Cambridge Hymnal*

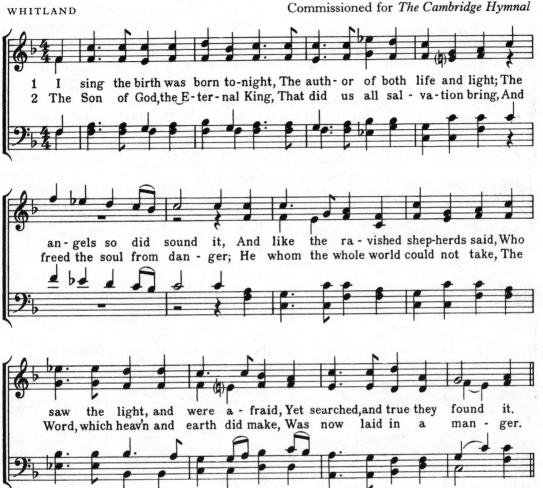

1 I sing the birth was born to-night, The auth- or of both life and light; The
2 The Son of God, the E-ter-nal King, That did us all sal - va-tion bring, And

an - gels so did sound it, And like the ra - vished shep-herds said, Who
freed the soul from dan - ger; He whom the whole world could not take, The

saw the light, and were a - fraid, Yet searched, and true they found it.
Word, which heav'n and earth did make, Was now laid in a man - ger.

1 I sing the birth was born tonight,
   The author both of life and light;
      The angels so did sound it,
   And like the ravished shepherds said,
   Who saw the light, and were afraid,
      Yet searched, and true they found it.

2 The Son of God, th' Eternal King,
   That did us all salvation bring,
      And freed the soul from danger;
   He whom the whole world could not take,
   The Word, which heaven and earth did make,
      Was now laid in a manger.

3 The Father's wisdom willed it so,
   The Son's obedience knew no No,
      Both wills were in one stature;
   And as that wisdom had decreed,
   The Word was now made flesh indeed,
      And took on Him our nature.

4 What comfort by him do we win?
   Who made himself the price of sin,
      To make us heirs of glory!
   To see this Babe, all innocence,
   A martyr born in our defence –
      Can man forget this story?

Ben Jonson, 1572–1637

JESUS BORN IN BETH'NY

Traditional melody from Virginia
Collected, John Jacob Niles, arranged E. P.

1 Je-sus born in Beth-'ny,__ Je-sus born in Beth-'ny,__
2 Je-sus went a-preach-in',__ Je-sus went a-preach-in',__
3 Ju-das did be-tray him, Ju-das did be-tray him,

Je-sus born in Beth-'ny, and in a man-ger lay;
Je-sus went a-preach-in' the Gos-pel of his God;
Ju-das did be-tray him and sold him for a bribe;

In a man-ger lay,____ in a man-ger lay,
Gos-pel of his Fa-ther, Gos-pel of his God,
Sold him for a bribe,____ sold him for a bribe,

Je - sus born in Beth - 'ny, and in a man - ger lay.
Je - sus went a - preach - in' the Gos - pel of his God.
Ju - das did be - tray him and sold him for a bribe.

4 They did cru - ci - fy him, They did cru - ci - fy__ him,
8 Ma - ry came a - weep - ing, Ma - ry came a - weep - ing,

They did cru - ci - fy him and nailed him to the tree;
Ma - ry came a - weep - ing, 'They've stole my Lord a - way;

20. (continued)

Nailed him to the tree,____ nailed him to the tree,
Stole my Lord a - way,____ stole my Lord a - way,'

They did cru - ci - fy him and nailed him to the tree;
Ma - ry came a - weep - ing, 'They've stole my Lord a - way.'

5 Jo-seph begged his bo - dy, Jo-seph begged his bo - dy, Jo-seph begged his
7 Ear-ly then one morn-ing, ear-ly then one morn-ing, Ear-ly then one

20 (continued)

Burst the bonds of death,___ burst the bonds of death,
Gone to Ga - li - lee,___ gone to Ga - li - lee,
To his Fa-ther's throne,___ to his Fa-ther's throne,

Tomb it would not hold him, it burst the bonds of death.
Je - sus has a - ris - en and gone to Ga - li - lee.
Je - sus then as - cend - ed up to his Fa-ther's throne.

By permission of G. Schirmer Inc., New York.
(Chappell & Co. Ltd., London).

1 Jesus born in Beth'ny, Jesus born in Beth'ny,
Jesus born in Beth'ny, and in a manger lay;
In a manger lay, in a manger lay,
Jesus born in Beth'ny, and in a manger lay.

2 Jesus went a-preachin', Jesus went a-preachin',
Jesus went a-preachin' the Gospel of his God;
Gospel of his Father, Gospel of his God,
Jesus went a-preachin' the Gospel of his God.

3 Judas did betray him, Judas did betray him,
Judas did betray him and sold him for a bribe;
Sold him for a bribe, sold him for a bribe,
Judas did betray him and sold him for a bribe.

4 They did crucify him, they did crucify him,
They did crucify him and nailed him to the tree;
Nailed him to the tree, nailed him to the tree,
They did crucify him and nailed him to the tree.

5 Joseph begged his body, Joseph begged his body,
Joseph begged his body and placed it in a tomb;
Placed it in a tomb, placed it in a tomb,
Joseph begged his body and placed it in a tomb.

6 Tomb it would not hold him, tomb it would not hold him,
Tomb it would not hold him, it burst the bonds of death;
Burst the bonds of death, burst the bonds of death,
Tomb it would not hold him, it burst the bonds of death.

7 Early then one morning, early then one morning,
Early then one morning, before the break of day,
Came a heavenly angel, rolled the stone away,
Early then one morning, before the break of day.

8 Mary came a-weeping, Mary came a-weeping,
Mary came a-weeping, 'They've stole my Lord away;
Stole my Lord away, stole my Lord away.'
Mary came a-weeping, 'They've stole my Lord away.'

9 Jesus has arisen, Jesus has arisen,
Jesus has arisen, and gone to Galilee;
Gone to Galilee, gone to Galilee,
Jesus has arisen and gone to Galilee.

10 Jesus then ascended, Jesus then ascended,
Jesus then ascended up to his Father's throne;
To his Father's throne, to his Father's throne,
Jesus then ascended up to his Father's throne.

Traditional, Virginia
Verses 3 and 4 modified in this edition.

21 CHRISTMAS DAY

Elizabeth Poston, 1905–

1 Last night in the open shippen[1]
   The infant Jesus lay,
   While cows stood at the hay-crib
   Twitching the sweet hay.

2 As I trudged through the snow-fields
   That lay in their own light,
   A thorn bush with its shadow
   Stood doubled on the night.

3 And I stayed on my journey
   To listen to the cheep
   Of a small bird in the thorn-bush
   I woke from its puffed sleep.

4 The bright stars were my angels
   And with the heavenly host
   I sang praise to the Father,
   The Son and Holy Ghost.

[1] *shippen* = cattle-shed.

Andrew Young, 1885–1971

22 LULLAY, LULLAY, THOU LYTIL CHILD

ALAN RIDOUT, 1934–
Commissioned for *The Cambridge Hymnal*

1 Lullay, lullay, thou lytil child,
  Sleep and be well still;
  The King of bliss thy father is,
  As it was his will.

2 This other night I saw a sight,
  A maid a cradle keep:
  'Lullay,' she sung, and said among,
  'Lie still, my child, and sleep.'

3 'How should I sleep? I may not for weep,
  So sore I am begone:
  Sleep I would; I may not for cold,
  And clothes have I none.

4 'For Adam's guilt mankind is spilt
  And that me rueth sore;
  For Adam and Eve here shall I live
  Thirty winter and more.'

'*Early English Carols*,' ed. R. L. Greene
15th century. From a MS. in Cambridge University Library. (*Add.* 5943)

53

LULLAY MY LIKING

Gustav Holst, 1874–1934

REFRAIN
Allegretto

Lul - lay my lik - ing, my dear son, my sweet - ing;

Lul - lay my dear heart, mine own dear dar - ling!

SOLO (1st verse)

1 I saw a fair maid - en Sit - ten and sing: She

lul - led a lit - tle child, A sweet - è loud - ing:

REFRAIN

SOLO (2nd verse)

2 That e - ter - nal lord is he That made al - lè thing; Of

al - lè lord - es he is Lord, Of al - lè king - ès King:

REFRAIN

SOLO (3rd verse)

3 There was mic - kle mel - o - dy At that child - ès birth: Al - though

they were in hea - ven's bliss They ma - dè mic - kle mirth:

REFRAIN

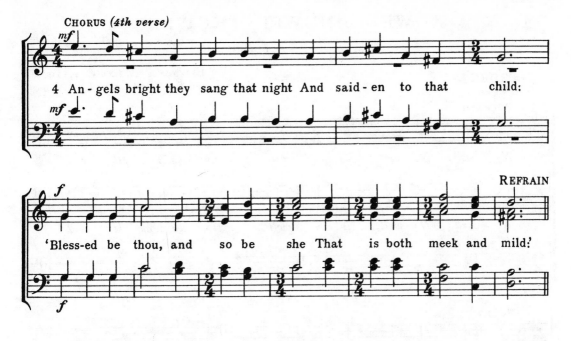

CHORUS (*4th verse*)

4 An-gels bright they sang that night And said-en to that child:

REFRAIN

'Bless-ed be thou, and so be she That is both meek and mild.'

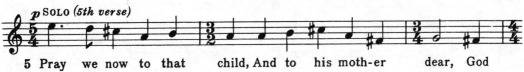

p SOLO (*5th verse*)

5 Pray we now to that child, And to his moth-er dear, God

REFRAIN

grant them all his bless-ing That now mak-en cheer:

Copyright, 1919, by J. Curwen & Sons Ltd.
By permission, from Curwen Edition No. 80589, published by J. Curwen & Sons Ltd., London.

Lullay my liking, my
  dear son, my sweeting;
Lullay my dear heart, mine
  own dear darling!

1 I saw a fair maiden
    Sitten and sing:
  She lullèd a little child,
    A sweetè lording:

2 That eternal lord is he
    That made allè thing;
  Of allè lordès he is Lord,
    Of allè kingès King:

3 There was a mickle melody
    At that childès birth:
  Although they were in heaven's bliss
    They madè mickle mirth:

4 Angels bright they sang that night
    And saiden to that child:
  'Blessed be thou, and so be she
    That is both meek and mild':

5 Pray we now to that child,
    And to his mother dear,
  God grant them all his blessing
    That now maken cheer:

Sloane MS. 15*th century*

24 NOWELL, NOWELL, NOWELL

3-part unacc. (S.A.T. and/or B)

ELIZABETH MACONCHY, 1907–
Commissioned for *The Cambridge Hymnal*

1 In Beth - le - hem in that fair ci - ty, A
2 Chil - dren were slain in full great plen - ty

is come. 1 In Beth - le - hem in that fair ci - ty, A
2 Chil - dren were slain in full great plen - ty

rex pa - ci - fi - cus is come.

child was born of a mai - den free, That shall a lord and
Je - su, for the love of thee; Where - fore their soul - ès

child was born of a mai - den free, That shall a lord and
Je - su, for the love of thee; Where - fore their soul - ès

BURDEN

prin - cè be; *A so - lis or - tus car - di - ne.* No - well, No -
sav - èd be; *Hos - tis He - ro - dis im - pi - e.* No - well, No -

prin - cè be; *A so - lis or - tus car - di - ne.* No - well, No -
sav - èd be; *Hos - tis He - ro - dis im - pi - e.* No - well, No -

No - well, No - well, No - well, No -

57

well, sing we now all and some.___ For rex pa-ci-fi-cus___

well, sing we now all and some, No-well, No-well, No-well, For

well, No-well, No-well sing we now all and some.___

to ⅏ last time

___ is come.___

3 As the sun-nė shin - eth through the glass, So
4 Now God is com-en to wor-ship-en us;

rex pa-ci-fi-cus___ is come. 3 As the sun - nė shin - eth through the glass, So
4 Now God is com-en to wor-ship-en us;

___ For rex pa-ci-fi-cus___ is come.___

Je - su in__ his mo - ther was;__ Thee to ser - vẻ now
Now of Ma - ry is born Je - sus;__ Make we mer - ry a -

Je - su in__ his mo - ther was; Thee to ser - vẻ now
Now of Ma - ry is born Je - sus; Make we mer - ry a -

BURDEN

grant us grace; *O lux be - a - ta Tri - ni - tas.*_____ } *No-well, No -*
mong - ẻs us; *Ex - ul - tet coe - lum lau - di - bus.*_____ } *No-well, No -*

grant us grace; *O lux be - a - ta Tri - ni - tas.*_____ } *No-well, No -*
mong - ẻs us; *Ex - ul - tet coe - lum lau - di - bus.*_____ } *No-well, No -*

*No - well, No - well, No - well,*_____ *No -*

59

Nowell, Nowell, Nowell
sing we now all and some,
For rex pacificus[1] is come.

1 In Bethlehem in that fair city,
A child was born of a maiden free;
That shall a lord and princè be;
A solis ortus cardine.[2]

2 Children were slain in full great plenty,
Jesus, for the love of thee;
Wherefore their soulès savèd be;
Hostis Herodis impie.[3]

3 As the sunnè shineth through the glass,
So Jesu in his mother was;
Thee to servè now grant us grace;
O lux beata Trinitas.[4]

4 Now God is comen to worshipen[5] us;
Now of Mary is born Jesus;
Make we merry amongès us;
Exultet coelum laudibus.[6]

Trinity College, Cambridge, MS. 0.3.58, late 15th century
From a collection of English songs and hymns, by James Ryman, a Franciscan friar.
Printed in 'Musica Britannica,' ed. J. Stevens, 1958

[1] The King of peace.
[2] From the rising point of the sun.
[3] Herod, ungodly enemy.
[4] O Light, blessed Trinity.
[5] *worshipen* = bless.
[6] Let the sky exult with praises.

25 BALULALOW
(O My Deir Heart)

Traditional Scots
Arranged, E. P.

© Elizabeth Poston

1 O my deir heart, young Jesus sweet,
Prepare thy cradle in my spreit;
And I sall rock thee in my heart,
And nevermair from thee depart.

2 But I sall praise thee evermore
With sangès sweet unto thy gloir;
The knees of my heart sall I bow,
And sing that richt *Balulalow!*

T. Wedderburn, 1567
From 'Ane Sang of the Birth of Christ,'
from 'Ane Compendious Buik of Godly and Spirituell Sangis,' 1567,
by James Wedderburn (1495?–1553), John Wedderburn (1500?–1556),
and Robert Wedderburn (1510?–1557?). The poem is a translation of a
Christmas carol by Martin Luther (1483–1546), from 'Geistliche Lieder' (1535)

ADESTE FIDELES

Music in the MS. of J. F. Wade, 1711–86
Descant, E. P.

DESCANT (*verse 3*)

1 Adeste fideles,
  Laeti triumphantes,
  Venite, venite in Bethlehem;
    Natum videte
    Regem angelorum:

    Venite adoremus,
    Venite adoremus,
    Venite adoremus Dominum.

2 Deum de Deo,
  Lumen de Lumine,
  Gestant puellae viscera;
    Deum verum
    Genitum non factum:

3 Cantet nunc io
  Chorus angelorum,
  Cantet nunc aula caelestium;
    Gloria
    In excelsis Deo:

4 Ergo qui natus
  Die hodierna,
  Jesu tibi sit gloria;
    Patris aeterni
    Verbum caro factum:

1 O come, all ye faithful,
  Joyful and triumphant,
  O come ye, O come ye to Bethlehem;
    Come and behold him,
    Born the King of angels:

    O come, let us adore him,
    O come, let us adore him,
    O come, let us adore him, Christ the Lord.

2 God of God,
  Light of Light,
  Lo, he abhors not the Virgin's womb;
    Very God,
    Begotten, not created:

3 Sing, choirs of angels,
  Sing in exultation,
  Sing, all ye citizens of heaven above;
    Glory to God
    In the highest:

4 Yea, Lord, we greet thee,
  Born this happy morning,
  Jesu, to thee be glory given;
    Word of the Father,
    Now in flesh appearing:

Hymn on the Prose for Christmas Day, ascribed to J. F. Wade, 1711–86

27

Sussex traditional, collected and arranged, R. Vaughan Williams (1872–1958)
Adapted, E. Harold Geer

News of great joy,— news of— great mirth,
When from our sin— he set— us free,
An - gels and men— with joy— may sing,
'Glo - ry to God— and peace to men,

News of our mer - ci - ful— King's birth.—
All for 'to gain our li - ber - ty.—
All for to see the new - born King.—
Now and for ev - er - more. A - men.'—

By permission of Stainer & Bell Ltd.

1 On Christmas night all Christians sing,
   To hear the news the angels bring;
   News of great joy, news of great mirth,
   News of our merciful King's birth.

2 Then why should men on earth be so sad,
   Since our Redeemer made us glad,
   When from our sin he set us free,
   All for to gain our liberty.

3 When sin departs before his grace,
   Then life and health come in its place;
   Angels and men with joy may sing,
   All for to see the new-born King.

4 All out of darkness we have light,
   Which made the angels sing this night:
   'Glory to God and peace to men,
   Now and for evermore. Amen.'

Traditional

28

QUI CREAVIT COELUM

Metrical rhythm
Harmonized by ANTHONY MILNER, 1925–
Commissioned for *The Cambridge Hymnal*

Free rhythm
Harmonized by ANTHONY MILNER

By, by, by,_____ by, by, Rex qui re-git se-cu-lum, Lul-ly, lul-ly, lu.

By, by, by, by, by,_____ Rex qui re-git se-cu-lum, Lul-ly, lul-ly, lu._____

or:

1 Qui creavit coelum,[1]
   Lully, lully, lu,
   Nascitur in stabulo,[2]
   By, by, by, by, by,
   Rex qui regit seculum,[3]
   Lully, lully, lu.

2 Joseph emit panniculum,[4]
   Lully, lully, lu,
   Mater involvit puerum,[5]
   By, by, by, by, by,
   Et ponit in presepio,[6]
   Lully, lully, lu.

3 Inter animalia,[7]
   Lully, lully, lu,
   Jacent mundi gaudia,[8]
   By, by, by, by, by,
   Dulcis super omnia,[9]
   Lully, lully, lu.

4 Lactat mater domini,[10]
   Lully, lully, lu,
   Osculatur parvulum,[11]
   By, by, by, by, by,
   Et adorat dominum,[12]
   Lully, lully, lu.

5 Roga mater filium,[13]
   Lully, lully, lu,
   Ut det nobis gaudium,[14]
   By, by, by, by, by,
   In perenni gloria,[15]
   Lully, lully, lu.

6 In sempiterna secula,[16]
   Lully, lully, lu,
   In eternum et ultra,[17]
   By, by, by, by, by,
   Det nobis sua gaudia,[18]
   Lully, lully, lu,
(Spoken) Puer natus est nobis![19]

Chester MS., c. 1425. *'The Processional of the Nuns of Chester,'*
ed. J. Wickham Legg, 1899, *for the Henry Bradshaw Society (No. XVIII)*

[1] He who created the heavens
[2] Is born in a stable
[3] The King who rules the ages
[4] Joseph buys a little shawl
[5] Mary swaddles her child
[6] And puts him in a manger
[7] Among the animals
[8] Lie the joys of the world
[9] Sweet above all things
[10] The mother of the Lord feeds him

[11] She kisses the little one
[12] And adores her lord
[13] Mother pray your son
[14] That he shall give us bliss
[15] Glory (to him) for ever
[16] World without end
[17] For ever and ever
[18] May he give us his joys
[19] Unto us a son is born

29 SING, ALL MEN

Kentucky Folk Carol, collected John Jacob Niles
Arranged, E. P.

Fast and light ♩ = 138

1 Sing, all men! 'tis Christ-mas morn-ing,
2 Come ye brave, and come ye strong, Re-

Je - sus Christ the Son's a - born-ing.
pent your sins, give up the wrong.

REFRAIN

Heigh, the hol - ly!
Ho, the heath - er! Ca - rol voic - es all to - geth - er!

p 3 In the man - ger all a - lone, The vir - gin moth - er
mp 4 Seek not earth - ly pow'r and pelf, But thro' your Je - sus

did a - tone.___ } Heigh, the hol - ly! Ho, the heath - er!
save your - self.___

Ca - rol voic - es all to - geth - er! *mp* 5 See the ox and
p 6 He who came on

see the kine, And see a - far the heav'n - ly sign.___
earth so low,___ Soon to man's e - state will grow.___

REFRAIN
Heigh, the hol - ly! Ho, the heath - er! Ca - rol voic - es all to - geth - er!

69

By permission of G. Schirmer Inc., New York
(Chappell & Co. Ltd., London)

1 Sing, all men! 'tis Christmas morning,
Jesus Christ the Son's a-borning.

Heigh, the holly! Ho, the heather!
Carol voices all together!

2 Come ye brave, and come ye strong,
Repent your sins, give up the wrong

3 In the manger all alone,
The virgin mother did atone.

4 Seek not earthly power and pelf,
But thro' your Jesus save yourself.

5 See the ox and see the kine,
And see afar the heavenly sign.

6 He who came on earth so low,
Soon to man's estate will grow.

7 And upon the cruel tree,
Will die in place of you and me.

Kentucky, traditional

30 SWEET WAS THE SONG
(Virgin's Lullaby)

Stanley Taylor, 1902–72
This arrangement commissioned for *The Cambridge Hymnal*

Andante con moto e legatissimo ♩ = 132
Gently—following the rise and fall of phrase

Lul - la, lul - la, lul - la, lul - la,

Sweet was the song the Vir - gin sung, When she to Beth - lem

lul - la, lul - la, lul - la,

Ju - da came, And was de - liv - ered of a Son, That

lul - la - by;

lul - la -

74

By courtesy of J. Curwen & Sons Ltd.

Sweet was the song the Virgin sung,
When she to Bethlem Juda came,
And was delivered of a Son,
That blessèd Jesus hath to name.
'Lulla, lulla, lulla, lullaby, sweet Babe,' sang she,
'My Son and eke a Saviour born,
Who hast vouchsafèd from on high
To visit us that were forlorn.'
'Lalula, lalula, lalulaby, sweet Babe,' sang she,
And rocked Him sweetly on her knee.

From William Ballet's Lute Book, 17th century;
MS. in Trinity College, Dublin

31 THAT LORD THAT LAY IN ASSÈ STALL

IMOGEN HOLST, 1907–
Commissioned for *The Cambridge Hymnal*

1 That Lord that lay in as-sè stall, Came to die for us all, To make us free that erst were thrall,—
Qui na-tus fu—it ho-di-e.

4 Now bless-èd be this Lord be-nign, That nold his cru-el death re-sign, But for—man-kind to die un-dign,—

REFRAIN

Qui na-tus fu—it, Qui na-tus fu—it ho-di-e, ho-di-e. Fine

ho——di-e. na—tus fu—it ho-di-e.

TENORS & BASSES

2 Well may we glad and mer-ry be, Since we were thrall and now be free; The

1 That Lord that lay in assè stall,
Came to die for us all,
To make us free that erst were thrall,
Qui natus fuit hodie.[1]

2 Well may we glad and merry be,
Since we were thrall and now be free;
The fiend our foe he made to flee,
Qui natus fuit hodie.

3 And since our foe is fled from us,
We may well sing and say right thus:
'Welcome he be, this Lord Jesus,
Qui natus fuit hodie.'

4 Now blessèd be this Lord benign,
That nold[2] his cruel death resign,
But for mankind to die undign,[3]
*Qui **natus** fuit hodie.*

15th century. Bodleian Library
MS. Arch. Selden B 26, printed in 'Lyrics of the Fifteenth Century,'
Carleton Brain, p. 118.

[1] Who was born today
[2] *nold* = would not
[3] *undign* = unworthy

COVERDALE'S CAROL

R. VAUGHAN WILLIAMS, 1872–1958 (in *Hodie*)

Andante sostenuto ♩ = 100
P dolce

1 The bless- ed son__ of God__ on- ly In a crib full__ poor__ did lie;__ With our__ poor flesh and our poor blood Was clothed that ev- er - last - ing good.__ Ky - ri - e - lei - son.
Lord have mer - cy.

2 The Lord Christ Je - su, God's son__ dear, Was a guest and a stran - ger here;__ Us for to

bring from mi-se-ry,___ That we___ might live___ e-

ter-nal-ly.___ { Ky-ri-e-lei-son.___ / Lord have mer-cy.___

pp
3 All this did he for us free-ly,
p cantabile
3 All this did he for us free-ly,

For to de-clare his great mer-cy;___ All Christ-en-dom be

mer-ry there-fore, And give him thanks for ev-er-more,___

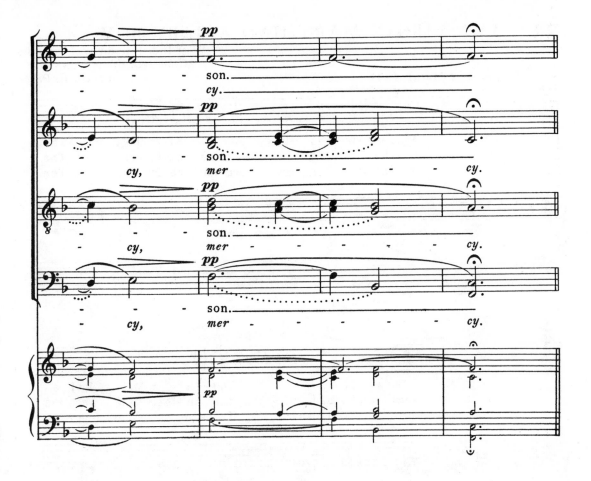

1 The blessed son of God only
    In a crib full poor did lie;
    With our poor flesh and our poor blood
    Was clothed that everlasting good.
        Kyrieleison.

2 The Lord Christ Jesu, God's son dear,
    Was a guest and a stranger here;
    Us for to bring from misery,
    That we might live eternally.
        Kyrieleison.

3 All this he did for us freely,
    For to declare his great mercy;
    All Christendom be merry therefore,
    And give him thanks for evermore.
        Kyrieleison.

Miles Coverdale (1487–1568) *after Martin Luther*

33 THE VIRGIN MARY HAD A BABY BOY

West Indian traditional carol
Collected, EDRIC CONNOR
Arranged, E. P.

Bright and joyful ♩=72

1 The Vir-gin Ma-ry had a ba-by boy, The
2 The an-gels sang when the ba-by born, The
3 The wise men saw when the ba-by born, The

Vir-gin Ma-ry had a ba-by boy, The Vir-gin Ma-ry had a
an-gels sang when the ba-by born, The an-gels sang_ when the
wise men saw where the ba-by born, The wise men went_ where the

cresc.

ba-by boy,
ba-by born, } And they say that his name was Je-sus.
ba-by born,

Words and melody reprinted from the Edric Connor Collection of West Indian Spirituals and Folk Tunes by permission of Boosey & Hawkes Music Publishers Ltd.

THE VIRGIN MARY HAD A BABY BOY

1 The Virgin Mary had a baby boy,[1]
  The Virgin Mary had a baby boy,
  The Virgin Mary had a baby boy,
  And they say that his name was Jesus.

  He come from the glory,
  He come from the glorious kingdom;
  He come from the glory,
  He come from the glorious kingdom;

  Oh, yes! Believer;
  Oh, yes! Believer;
  He come from the glory,
  He come from the glorious kingdom.

2 The angels sang when the baby born,[2]
  And proclaim him the Saviour Jesus.

3 The wise men saw when the baby born,
  The wise men saw where the baby born,
  The wise men went where the baby born,
  And they say that his name was Jesus.

West Indian traditional, collected by Edric Connor

[1] In the original 'De Virgin Mary'.
[2] In the original, 'De baby born'.
Taken down from the singing of the Negro James Bryce in 1942 when Bryce was 92 years old.

34 THERE IS NO ROSE OF SUCH VIRTUE

Anonymous, *c.* 1420
Transcribed and edited by John Stevens

Printed by permission of the Royal Musical Association

The melody lines of this carol are apt for voice and instrument and are interchangeable; the lower melody and its adjoining part may also be sung an octave higher in the treble clef. An optional 'mean' or middle part, added by the editor, is printed in small notes.

> *There is no rose of such virtue,*
> *As is the rose that bare Jesu.*

1 There is no rose of such virtue
As is the rose that bare Jesu;
Alleluia.

2 For in this rose contained was
Heaven and earth in little space;
Res miranda.[1]

3 By that rose we may well see
That he is God in persons three,
Pari forma.[2]

4 The angels sungen the shepherds to:
Gloria in excelsis Deo:
Gaudeamus.[3]

5 Leave we all this worldly mirth,
And follow we this joyful birth;
Transeamus.[4]

15th century. Trinity College, Cambridge, MS. 0.3.58

[1] Marvellous thing
[2] Of equal form
[3] Let us rejoice
[4] Let us go across (from worldly to heavenly things)

35 THERE IS NO ROSE OF SUCH VIRTUE

Anonymous, *c.* 1420
Transcribed and edited by John Stevens

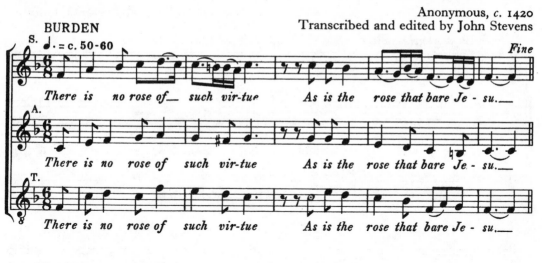

© Copyright 1963 by Stainer & Bell Ltd.   *Printed by permission*

Note by John Stevens:

From a MS. roll of carols, copied out in the early 15th century and now in the Library of Trinity College, Cambridge; printed by kind permission. The carol begins and ends with the chorus (the alto part is editorial and may be omitted at will); the verses are for soloists. Small accidentals in the chorus are absent from the MS. and may be ignored if you wish. The tenor has the tune throughout, and the other voices should be subordinate. The music was intended to be sung unaccompanied.

36 THIS ENDRIS NIGHT

English carol melody, 15th–16th century
Arranged, E. P.

With a gentle swing

This end - ris night I saw a sight, A star as bright as day; And ev - er a - mong, A maid - en sung, 'Lul - lay, by, by, lul - lay.'

MELODY

© Elizabeth Poston

1   This endris night[1]
     I saw a sight,
   A star as bright as day;
     And ever among,[2]
     A maiden sung,
   'Lullay, by, by, lullay.'

2   This lovely lady sat and sung,
     And to her child did say:
   'My son, my brother, father, dear,
     Why liest thou thus in hay?
   My sweetest bird, thus 'tis required,
     Though thou be king veray;[3]
   But nevertheless I will not cease
     To sing, By, by, lullay.'

3   The child then spake in his talking,
     And to his mother said:
   'Yea, I am known as heaven-king,
     In crib though I be laid;
   For angels bright down to me light:[4]
     Thou knowest 'tis no nay:[5]
   And for that sight thou may'st delight
     To sing, By, by, lullay.'

4   'Now sweet son, since thou art a king,
     Why art thou laid in stall?
   Why dost not order thy bedding
     In some great kingès hall?
   Methinks 'tis right that king or knight
     Should lie in good array:
   And then among, it were no wrong
     To sing, By, by, lullay.'

5   'Mary mother, I am thy child,
     Though I be laid in stall;
   For lords and dukes shall worship me,
     And so shall kingès all.
   Ye shall well see that Kingès three
     Shall come on this twelfth day,
   For this behest give me thy breast,
     And sing, By, by, lullay.'

6   'Now tell, sweet son, I thee do pray
     Thou art my love and dear –
   How should I keep thee to thy pay,[6]
     And make thee glad of cheer?
   For all thy will I would fulfil –
     Thou knowest well, in fay;[7]
   And for all this I will thee kiss,
     And sing, By, by, lullay.'

7   'My dear mother, when time it be,
     Take thou me up on loft,
   And set me then upon thy knee,
     And handle me full soft;
   And in thy arm thou hold me warm,
     And keep me night and day,
   And if I weep, and may not sleep,
     Thou sing, by, by, lullay.'

8   'Now sweet son, since it is come so,
     That all is at thy will,
   I pray thee grant to me a boon,
     If it be right and skill,[8] –
   That child or man, who will or can
     Be merry on my day,
   To bliss thou bring – and I shall sing,
     Lullay, by, by, lullay.'

Anon. 15th Century. Bodleian MS. Eng. Poet. e.l. and Balliol MS. 354
The 'Oxford Book of Carols' says: 'It was not new when it was written out in
the Bodleian MS. dated between 1460 and 1490.'

[1] The other night.   **2** *ever among* = every now and then.   [3] *veray* = true.   [4] *light* = alight.
[5] *no nay* = not to be denied.   [6] *pay* = satisfaction.   [7] *in fay* = in faith.   [8] *skill* = reasonable.

37 MY DANCING DAY
(UNACC.)

English Traditional
Arranged, E. P.

Lightly, with a dance pulse (one-in-a-bar stress) ♩.= 66

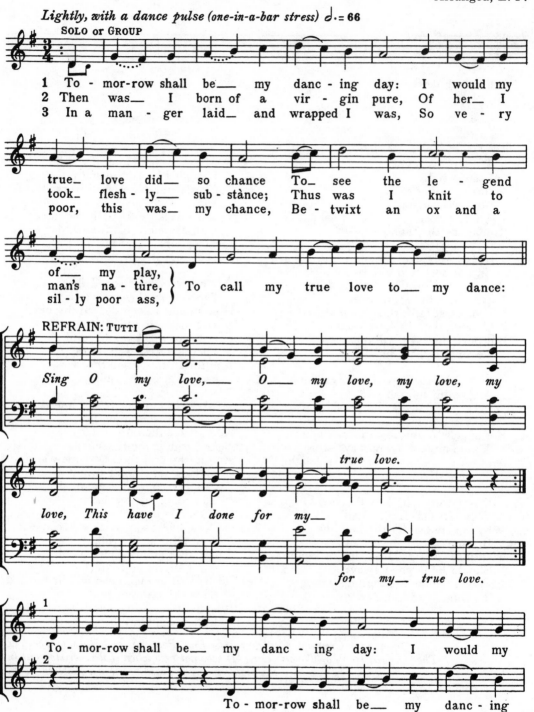

1 To - mor-row shall be__ my danc - ing day: I would my
2 Then was__ I born of a vir - gin pure, Of her__ I
3 In a man - ger laid__ and wrapped I was, So ve - ry

true__ love did__ so chance To see the le - gend
took__ flesh-ly__ sub - stance; Thus was I knit to
poor, this was__ my chance, Be - twixt an ox and a

of__ my play,
man's na - ture, } To call my true love to__ my dance:
sil - ly poor ass,

REFRAIN: TUTTI

Sing O my love,__ O__ my love, my love, my

true love.

love, This have I done for my__

for my__ true love.

1 To - mor-row shall be__ my danc - ing day: I would my

2 To - mor-row shall be__ my danc - ing

Either refrain, or both, may be used, in optional order

88

© Elizabeth Poston

1 Tomorrow shall be my dancing day:
   I would my true love did so chance
To see the legend of my play,
   To call my true love to my dance:
     Sing O my love, O my love, my love, my love;
     This have I done for my true love.

2 Then was I born of a virgin pure,
   Of her I took fleshly substance;
Thus was I knit to man's nature;
   To call my true love to my dance:

3 In a manger laid and wrapped I was,
   So very poor, this was my chance,
Betwixt an ox and a silly poor ass,
   To call my true love to my dance:

English traditional, from Sandys, 1833

MY DANCING DAY

(ACC.)

English traditional melody, from W. Sandys,
Christmas Carols Ancient and Modern, 1833
Arranged, E. P.

1 To-mor-row shall be— my danc-ing day: I would my true— love did— so chance To— see the le-gend of— my play, To call my true love to— my dance:

REFRAIN
ALL UNISON

Sing O my— love, O— my love, my love, my love; This have I done— for my— true love.

Lyrics:

2 Then was I born of a vir - gin pure, Of her I took flesh - ly sub - stance; Thus was I knit to man's na - ture, To call my true love to my dance:

* Or keyboard if without flute.

38 (continued)

REFRAIN: UNISON

Sing O my love, O my love, my love, my love, This have I done for my true love.

3 In a man - ger laid and wrapped I was, So ve - ry poor, this was my chance, Be -

twixt an ox and a sil-ly poor ass, To call my

Fl. tacet

REFRAIN

true_ love to_ my dance. *Sing O my_ love,*

O_ my love, my love, my love; This have I

Flute

Flute tacet

done for my_ true love._

4-PART or UNISON

To - mor - row shall be__ my danc - ing day: I would my

true__ love did__ so chance To see the le - gend

of__ my play, To call my true__ love to__ my dance:

REFRAIN: UNISON
poco f

Sing O my love, O my love, my love, my love, This have I done for my true love.

© Elizabeth Poston

1 Tomorrow shall be my dancing day:
   I would my true love did so chance
To see the legend of my play,
   To call my true love to my dance:
     Sing O my love, O my love, my love, my love;
     This have I done for my true love.

2 Then was I born of a virgin pure,
   Of her I took fleshly substance;
Thus was I knit to man's nature,
   To call my true love to my dance:

3 In a manger laid and wrapped I was,
   So very poor, this was my chance,
Betwixt an ox and a silly poor ass,
   To call my true love to my dance:

English traditional, from Sandys, 1833

WHAT TIDINGS BRING'ST US, MESSENGER?

15th-century carol tune, Trinity College, Cambridge, MS. o.3.58
Arranged ELIZABETH POSTON, 1905–

BURDEN
Joyous and flowing

Fine

What tid-ings bring'st us, mes-sen-ger, Of Christ-ès birth this New Year's Day?

1 A babe is born__ of high na-ture, A Prince of
2 A seem-ly sel-couth it is__ to see: The girl that
3 A won-der thing__ is now__ be-fall: That Lord that
4 This love-ly la-dy did greet her child: 'Hail son, hail
5 That Lord that all__ things made of naught Is man be -

Peace that ev-er shall be; Of heav'n and earth he__
hath__ this bairn y-borne, This child__ con-ceived in__
made__ both sea__ and sun,__ Heav'n and earth and__
bro-ther, hail fa-ther dear!' 'Hail daugh-ter, hail sis-ter, hail
come__ for man's__ love, For with__ his blood he__

hath the cure, His lord-ship is e - ter - ni - ty. Such
high de-gree, And maid - en is as was_ be - forne. Such
an - gels all,_ In man-kind is now_ be - come. What
mo - ther mild!' This hail - ing was in wise_ man - ner. Such
shall be bought From bale to bliss that is_ a - bove. Such

won - der tid - ings ye_ may hear: That God_ and man_ are
won - der tid - ings ye_ may hear: That maid-en and mo-ther is
tid - ings bring'st us, mes - sen - ger? A child that is_ but
won - der tid - ings ye_ may hear: This greet - ing was_ of
won - der tid - ings ye may now hear: That Lord us grant_

brought more near, Our sin had made us fiend - ès prey.
one_ crea - ture And la - dy is of high ar - ray.
of_ one year Ev - er has been and shall be aye.
so_ high cheer That man's pain it turned to play.
now_ our prayer, To dwell in heav - en that_ we may.

> *What tidings bring'st us, messenger,*
> *Of Christès birth this New Year's Day.*[1]

1 A babe is born of high nature,
    A Prince of Peace that ever shall be;
Of heaven and earth he hath the cure,[1]
    His lordship is eternity.
        Such wonder tidings ye may hear:
        That God and man are brought more near,
            Our sin had made us fiendès prey.

2 A seemly selcouth[2] it is to see:
    The girl that hath this bairn yborne,
This child conceived in high degree,
    And maiden is as was beforne.
        Such wonder tidings ye may hear:
        That maiden and mother is one creature
            And lady is of high array.

3 A wonder thing is now befall:
    That Lord that made both sea and sun,
Heaven and earth and angels all,
    In mankind is now become.
        What tidings bring'st us, messenger?
        A child that is but of one year
            Ever has been and shall be aye.

4 This lovely lady did greet her child:
    'Hail son, hail brother, hail father dear!'
'Hail daughter, hail sister, hail mother mild!'
    This hailing was in wise manner.
        Such wonder tidings ye may hear:
        This greeting was of so high cheer
            That man's pain it turned to play.

5 That Lord that all things made of naught
    Is man become for man's love,
For with his blood he shall be bought
    From bale to bliss that is above.
        Such wonder tidings ye may now hear:
        That Lord us grant now our prayer,
            To dwell in heaven that we may.

Burden and stanzas 1, 2, 3, 4: Trinity College, Cambridge, MS. 0.3.58
15th century. By John Audelay (?)
stanza 5: Bodleian Library MS.

---

[1] *cure* = spiritual charge, also the capacity to heal.
[2] *seemly selcouth* = marvellous ('seldom known') thing.

40

Este's *Psalter*, 1592

T. RAVENSCROFT in his *Psalter*, 1621

Melody in the Tenor
UNISON

1 While shepherds watched their flocks by night,
　All seated on the ground,
The angel of the Lord came down,
　And glory shone around.

2 'Fear not,' said he (for mighty dread
　Had seized their troubled mind);
'Glad tidings of great joy I bring
　To you and all mankind.

3 'To you in David's town this day
　Is born of David's line
A Saviour, who is Christ the Lord;
　And this shall be the sign:

4 'The heavenly babe you there shall find
　To human view displayed,·
All meanly wrapped in swathing[1] bands
　And in a manger laid.'

5 Thus spake the seraph; and forthwith
　Appeared a shining throng
Of angels praising God, who thus
　Addressed their joyful song:

6 'All glory be to God on high,
　And to the earth be peace;
Goodwill henceforth from heaven to men
　Begin and never cease.'

Nahum Tate, 1652--1715

[1] Pronounce 'swaything.'

41

WONDROUS LOVE

As harmonized in the original shape-note notation

Early American

What won-drous love is this, O my soul, O my
soul; What won-drous love is this, O my soul;____
What won-drous love is this That caused the Lord of
bliss To bear the dread-ful curse for my soul, for my

WONDROUS LOVE

1 What wondrous love is this, O my soul, O my soul;
What wondrous love is this, O my soul;
What wondrous love is this
That caused the Lord of bliss
To bear the dreadful curse for my soul, for my soul,
To bear the dreadful curse for my soul?

2 When I was sinking down, sinking down, sinking down,
When I was sinking down, sinking down,
When I was sinking down
Beneath God's righteous frown,
Christ laid aside his crown for my soul, for my soul,
Christ laid aside his crown for my soul.

3 To God and to the Lamb I will sing, I will sing;
To God and to the Lamb I will sing;
To God and to the Lamb
Who is the great I AM,
While millions join the theme, I will sing, I will sing,
While millions join the theme, I will sing.

4 And when from death I'm free, I'll sing on, I'll sing on;
And when from death I'm free, I'll sing on;
And when from death I'm free
I'll sing and joyful be,
And through eternity I'll sing on, I'll sing on;
And through eternity I'll sing on.

Anonymous, 1867

41 (continued)

DESCANT

won-drous love is this, O my soul; What won-drous love is

poco cresc.

this That caused the Lord of bliss To bear the dread-ful curse for my

soul, for my soul, To bear the dread-ful curse for my soul?

42

THAT VIRGIN'S CHILD

Edmund Rubbra, 1901–
Commissioned for *The Cambridge Hymnal*

LINDENS

Moderately slow

1 That vir-gin's child Most meek and mild, A-
2 Such pain and smart As in his heart He

lone-ly for my sake, His fa-ther's will For
suf-fered for man-kind Can no man take, Nor

to ful-fil He came great pains to take.
mourn-ing make So meek-ly for his friend.

THAT VIRGIN'S CHILD

1 That virgin's child
 Most meek and mild,
  Alonely for my sake,
 His father's will
 For to fulfil
  He came great pains to take.

2 Such pain and smart
 As in his heart
  He suffered for mankind
 Can no man take,
 Nor mourning make
  So meekly for his friend.

3 Now Christ Jesu,
 Of love most true,
  Have mercy upon me:
 I ask thee grace
 For my trespass,
  That I have done to thee.

4 For thy sweet name
 Save me from shame
  And all adversity:
 For Mary's sake
 To thee me take,
  And mourn no more for me.

John Gwyneth, c. 1530

43

JENA (DAS NEUGEBORNE KINDLEIN)

Melody from VULPIUS's *Gesangbuch* (Jena, 1609)
Harmonized and arranged with descant by E. P.

1 The ho - ly Son__ of God most high,__ For love of A - dam's
4 The Son of God__ thus man be - came, That men the sons of

lap - sèd__ race, Quit the sweet plea - sures of__ the sky__
God might be, And by their se - cond birth re - gain__

To bring us to__ that hap - py place. 2 His robes of light__ he
A like - ness to__ his de - i - ty.

p

MELODY

laid a - side,__ Which did his ma - jes - ty a - dorn,__ And the frail

state of mor - tals tried,__ In hu - man flesh and fi - gure born.

1 The holy Son of God most high,
    For love of Adam's lapsèd race,
    Quit the sweet pleasures of the sky
    To bring us to that happy place.

2 His robes of light he laid aside,
    Which did his majesty adorn,
    And the frail state of mortals tried,
    In human flesh and figure born.

3 Whole choirs of angels loudly sing
    The mystery of his sacred birth;
    And the blest news to shepherds bring,
    Filling their watchful souls with mirth.

4 The Son of God thus man became,
    That men the sons of God might be,
    And by their second birth regain
    A likeness to his deity.

Henry More, 1614–87

44 A NEW YEAR CAROL

Benjamin Britten, 1913–

1 Here we bring new wa-ter from the well so clear,
2 Sing reign of Fair Maid, with gold up-on her toe,
3 Sing reign of Fair Maid, with gold up-on her chin,

For to wor-ship God with, this hap-py New Year.
O-pen you the West Door, and turn the Old Year go.
O-pen you the East Door, and let the New Year in.

Sing

CHORUS (for verses 1 & 2)

le-vy dew, sing le-vy dew, the wa-ter and the wine; The

se-ven bright gold wires and the bu-gles that do shine.

CHORUS *(for verse 3)*

le - vy dew, sing le - vy dew, the wa-ter and the wine; The

se - ven bright gold wires and the bu-gles that do shine.

Copyright 1936 by Boosey & Co. Ltd.
Reprinted by permission of Boosey & Hawkes Music Publishers Ltd.

1 Here we bring new water from the well so clear,
  For to worship God with, this happy New Year.
    Sing levy dew, sing levy dew, the water and the wine;
    The seven bright gold wires and the bugles that do shine.

2 Sing reign of Fair Maid, with gold upon her toe,
  Open you the West Door, and turn the Old Year go.

3 Sing reign of Fair Maid, with gold upon her chin,
  Open you the East Door, and let the New Year in.

Traditional

107

45 TWELFTH NIGHT SONG

TWO-PART UNACC. WITH A
CONCLUDING ROUND FOR 4 VOICES

Elizabeth Maconchy, 1907–
Commissioned for *The Cambridge Hymnal*

45 (continued)

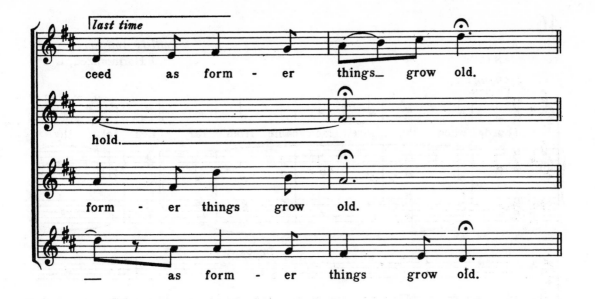

ceed as form - er things grow old.

hold.

form - er things grow old.

as form - er things grow old.

1 Down with the rosemary and bays,
    Down with the mistletoe;
Instead of holly, now upraise
    The greener box, for show.

2 The holly hitherto did sway:
    Let box now domineer
Until the dancing Easter day,
    Or Easter's eve appear.

3 The graceful box, which now hath grace
    Your houses to renew,
Grown old, surrender must his place
    Unto the crispèd yew.

4 When yew is out, then birch comes in,
    And many flowers beside,
Both of a fresh and fragrant kin,
    To honour Whitsuntide.

5 Green rushes then, and sweetest bents,
    With cooler oaken boughs,
Come in for comely ornaments,
    To re-adorn the house.

6 Thus times do shift; each thing his turn does hold;
New things succeed, as former things grow old.

Robert Herrick, 1591–1674

46

ST. VENANTIUS

Poitiers Antiphoner, 1746
Harmonized, E. P.

1 Lord, when the wise men came from far,
Led to thy cradle by a star,
Shepherds in humble fearfulness
Walked safely, though their light was less.

2 Wise men in tracing nature's laws
Ascend unto the highest cause:
Though wise men better know the way,
It seems no honest heart can stray.

3 And since no creature comprehends
The Cause of causes, End of ends,
He who himself vouchsafes to know
Best pleases his Creator so.

4 There is no merit in the wise
But love, the shepherds' sacrifice:
Wise men, all ways of knowledge past,
To the shepherds' wonder came at last.

Sidney Godolphin, 1610–43 *(altered)*

112

INDEX

Roman type is used for first lines; italics for titles. References are to song numbers.

A babe is born of high nature 39
A virgin most pure, as the prophets do tell 3
Adam lay ybounden 2
Adeste Fideles 26
All this night shrill chanticleer 4
Balulalow 25
Behold a silly tender babe 5
Boar's Head Carol, The 6
Chanticleer's Carol 4
Christmas Day 21
Corpus Christi Carol 7
Coverdale's Carol 32
Deo Gratias 2
Down in yon forest there stands a hall 7
Down with the rosemary and bays 45
Francis Kindlemarsh's Carol 9
From virgin's womb this Christmas day did
    spring 9
God rest you merry, Gentlemen 10
Hark, the herald-angels sing 11
Here we bring new water from the well so clear
    44
Hush! my dear, lie still and slumber 13
I saw a fair maiden 23
I sing of a maiden 14
I sing the birth was born tonight 19
In a field as I lay, methought I heard 15
In Bethlehem in that fair city 24
In the bleak mid-winter 16
Into this world this day did come 18
It was poor little Jesus 17
Jesus born in Beth'ny 20
Jesus Christ the Apple Tree 1
Last night in the open shippen 21
Lord, when the wise men came from far 46

Lullay, lullay, thou lytil child 22
Lullay My Liking 23
My Dancing Day 37, 38
New Year Carol, A 44
Nowell, Nowell, Nowell 24
O come, all ye faithful 26
O my deir heart, young Jesus sweet 25
On Christmas night all Christians sing 27
Poor Little Jesus 17
Qui Creavit Coelum 28
Sing, all men! 'tis Christmas morning 29
Sussex Carol, The 27
Sweet was the song the Virgin sung 30
That Lord that lay in assè stall 31
That Virgin's Child 42
The blessed son of God only 32
The boar's head in hand bear I 6
The first Nowell the angel did say 8
The holly and the ivy 12
The holy Son of God most high 43
The tree of life my soul hath seen 1
The Virgin Mary had a baby boy 33
There is no rose of such virtue 34, 35
This endris night 36
Tomorrow shall be my dancing day 37, 38
Twelfth Night Carol 24
Twelfth Night Song 45
Virgin's Lullaby 30
Watts's Cradle Song 13
What tidings bring'st us, messenger? 39
What wondrous love is this, O my soul 41
Where Riches Is Everlastingly 18
While shepherds watched their flocks by night
    40
Wondrous Love 41